POSITIVE DOODLES

STERLING
New York

An Imprint of Sterling Publishing
1166 Avenue of the Americas
New York, NY 10036

STERLING and the distinctive Sterling logo are registered trademarks of Sterling Publishing Co., Inc.

© 2016 by Emm Roy

ISBN 978-1-4549-1850-9

Distributed in Canada by Sterling Publishing
c/o Canadian Manda Group, 664 Annette Street
Toronto, Ontario, Canada M6S 2C8
Distributed in the United Kingdom by GMC Distribution Services
Castle Place, 166 High Street, Lewes, East Sussex, England BN7 1XU
Distributed in Australia by Capricorn Link (Australia) Pty. Ltd.
P.O. Box 704, Windsor, NSW 2756, Australia

For information about custom editions, special sales, and premium and corporate purchases,
please contact Sterling Special Sales at 800-805-5489 or specialsales@sterlingpublishing.com.

Manufactured in China

2 4 6 8 10 9 7 5 3 1

www.sterlingpublishing.com

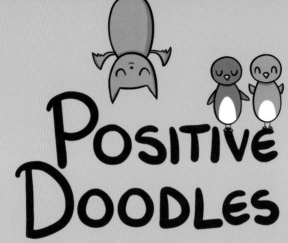

POSITIVE DOODLES

46 Good Thoughts for Good Friends

EMM ROY

STERLING
New York

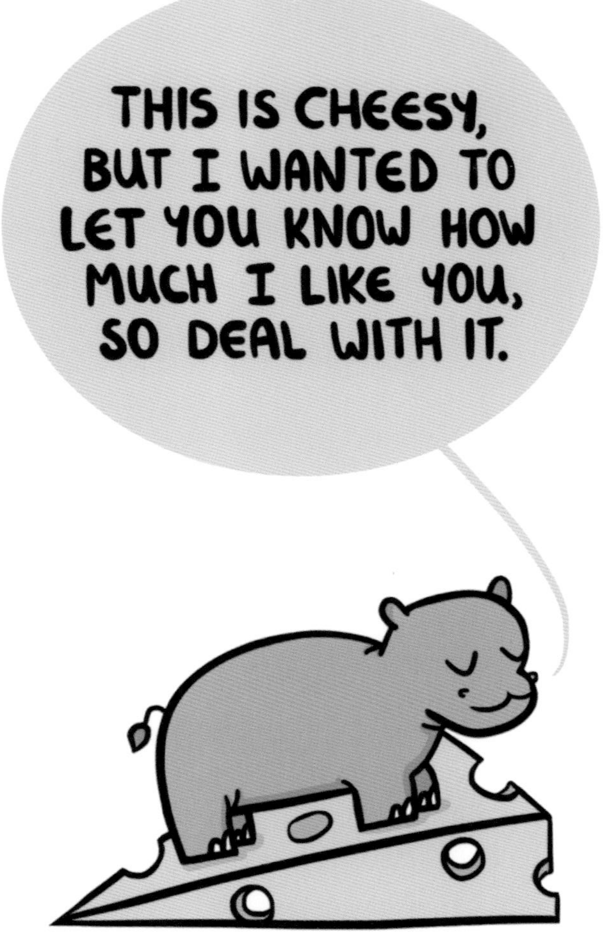
THIS IS CHEESY, BUT I WANTED TO LET YOU KNOW HOW MUCH I LIKE YOU, SO DEAL WITH IT.

POSITIVE
DOODLES

I LIKE YOU EVEN MORE THAN I LIKE NOT HAVING TO DO THINGS I DON'T WANT TO DO.

POSITIVE
DOODLES

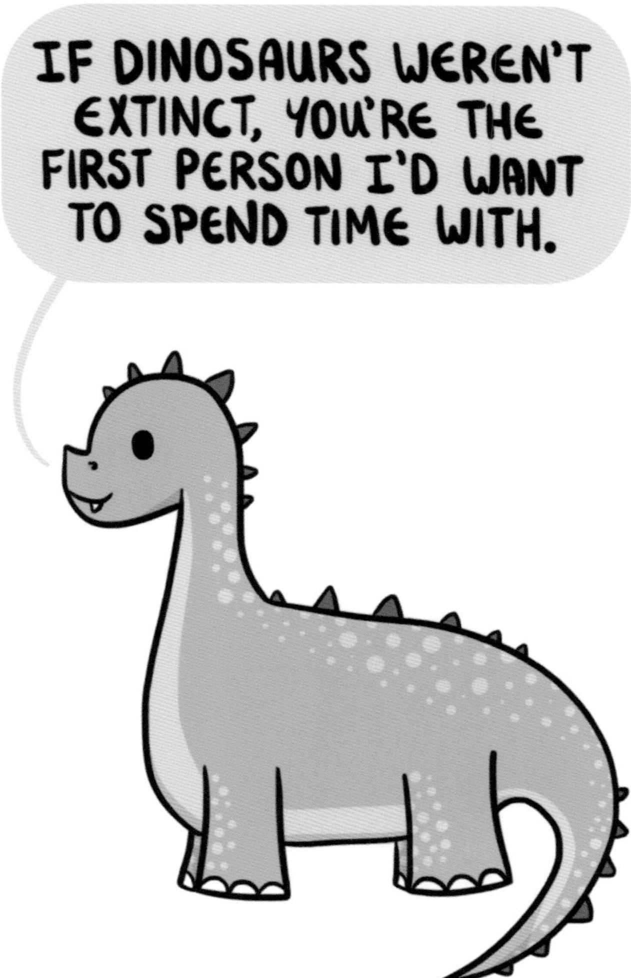
IF DINOSAURS WEREN'T EXTINCT, YOU'RE THE FIRST PERSON I'D WANT TO SPEND TIME WITH.

_____

_____

_____

_____

Positive
Doodles

I SUPPORT YOU IN ALL YOUR WEIRD ENDEAVORS.

_____

_____

_____

_____

PosITIVE
DoodLes

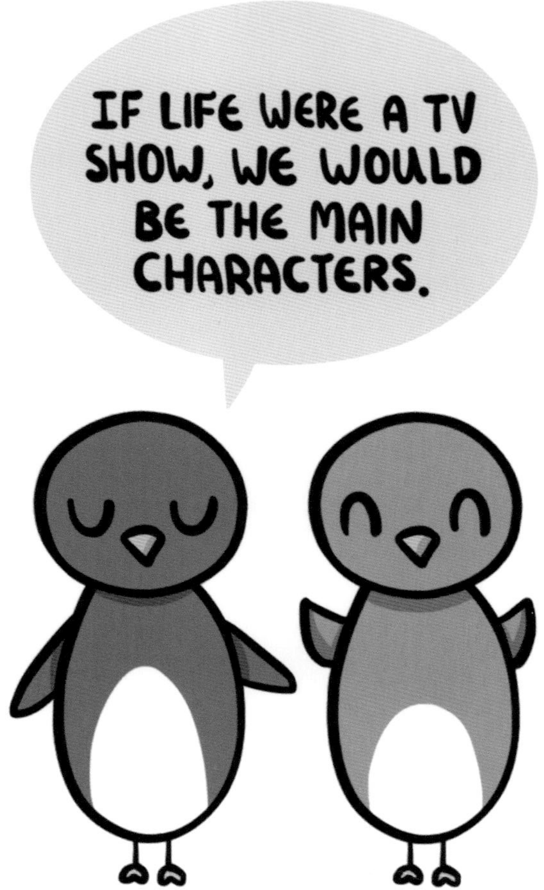
IF LIFE WERE A TV SHOW, WE WOULD BE THE MAIN CHARACTERS.

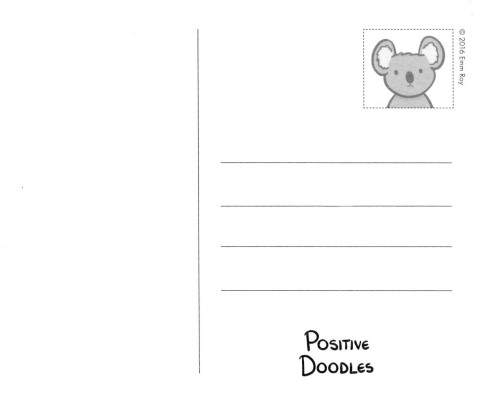

POSITIVE
DOODLES

YOU'RE GREAT AND
I LIKE YOU. JUST
DON'T EVER WAKE
ME UP WHEN I'M
TRYING TO SLEEP IN.

_____

_____

_____

_____

POSITIVE
DOODLES

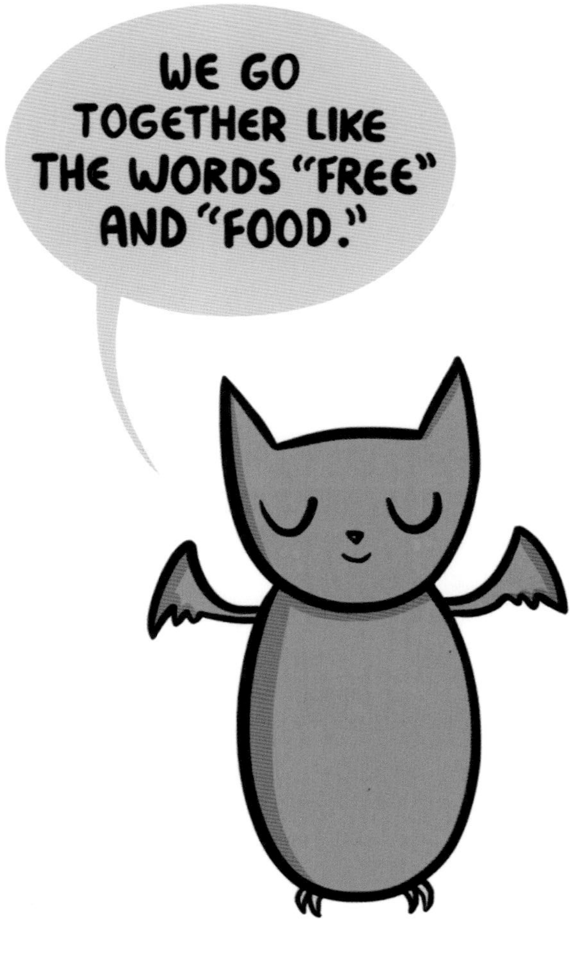
WE GO TOGETHER LIKE THE WORDS "FREE" AND "FOOD."

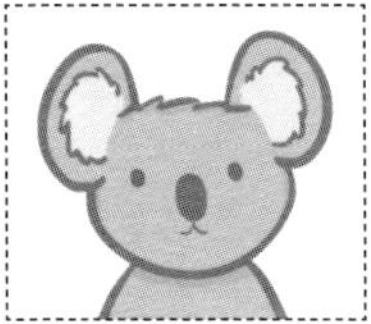

Positive Doodles

I LIKE YOU.
LET'S GET FOOD.

_____

_____

_____

_____

POSITIVE
DOODLES

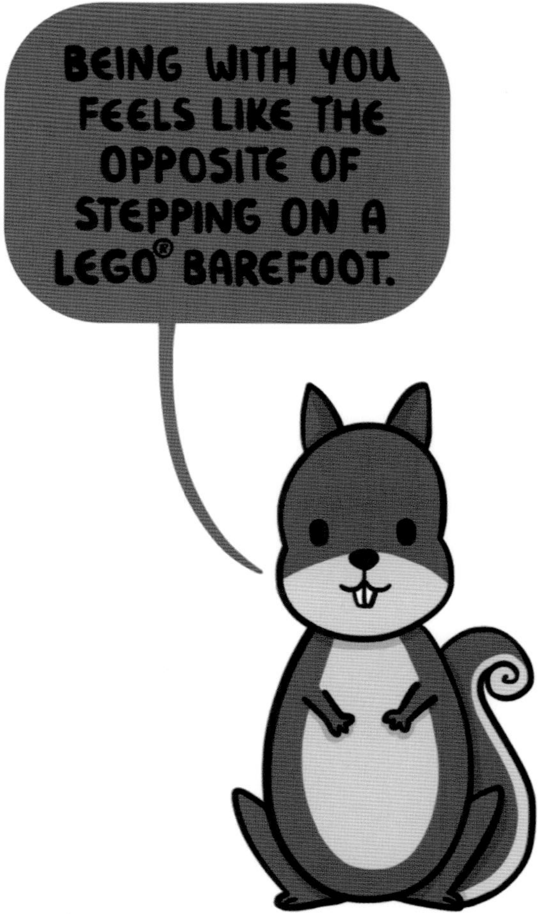
BEING WITH YOU FEELS LIKE THE OPPOSITE OF STEPPING ON A LEGO® BAREFOOT.

_____

_____

_____

_____

POSITIVE
DOODLES

IF I EVER TAKE OVER THE WORLD WITH SOMEONE, IT WILL BE YOU.

_____

_____

_____

_____

POSITIVE
DOODLES

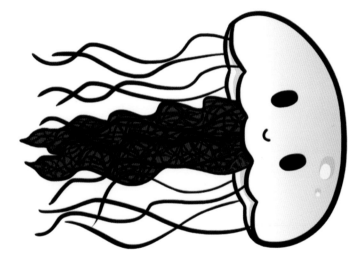

BORING THINGS SEEM TO MAGICALLY STOP BEING BORING WHEN I DO THEM WITH YOU.

Positive
Doodles

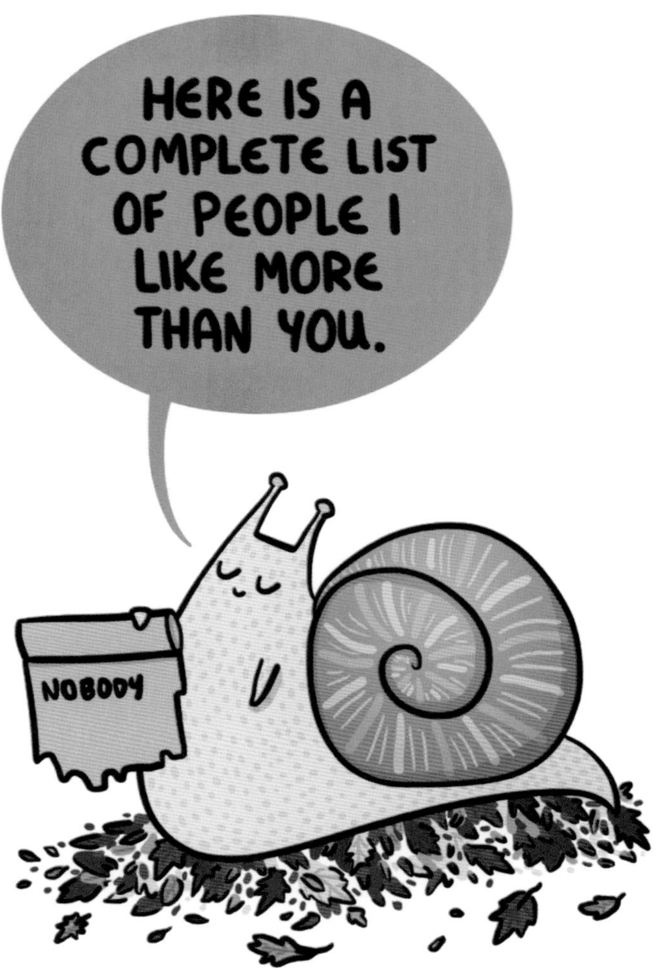
HERE IS A COMPLETE LIST OF PEOPLE I LIKE MORE THAN YOU.
NOBODY

_____

_____

_____

_____

Positive
Doodles

OTHER PEOPLE DON'T ALWAYS UNDERSTAND US, BUT WHO CARES? WE'RE HILARIOUS!

POSITIVE
DOODLES

MY FAVORITE THING ABOUT YOU IS THAT YOU UNDERSTAND HOW AMAZING I AM. MY SECOND FAVORITE THING ABOUT YOU IS EVERYTHING.

_____

_____

_____

_____

Positive
Doodles

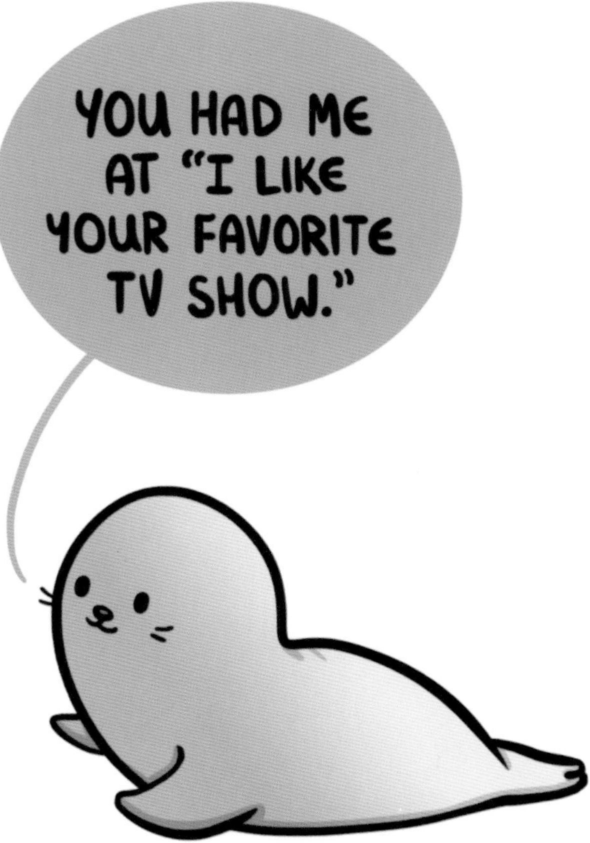
YOU HAD ME AT "I LIKE YOUR FAVORITE TV SHOW."

POSITIVE
DOODLES

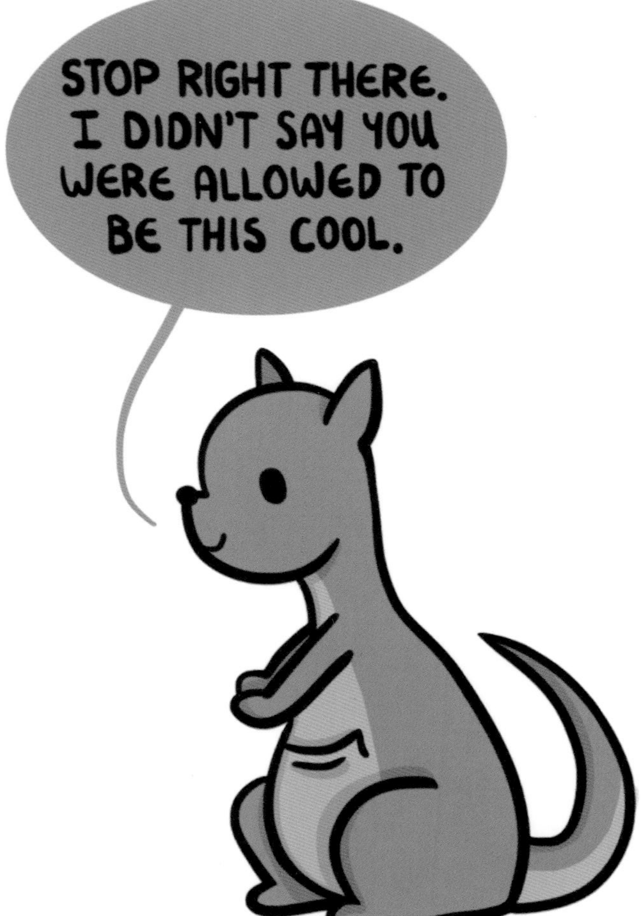
STOP RIGHT THERE. I DIDN'T SAY YOU WERE ALLOWED TO BE THIS COOL.

_____

_____

_____

_____

Positive
Doodles

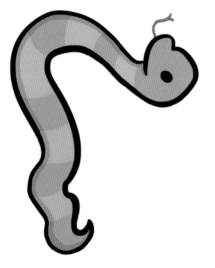

I LOVE HOW WE'RE SO CLOSE THAT YOU CAN ALWAYS TELL WHAT I'M THINKING. WELL, IT'S EITHER CLOSENESS OR YOU HAVE THE ABILITY TO READ MINDS. EITHER WAY, I LOVE IT.

Positive
Doodles

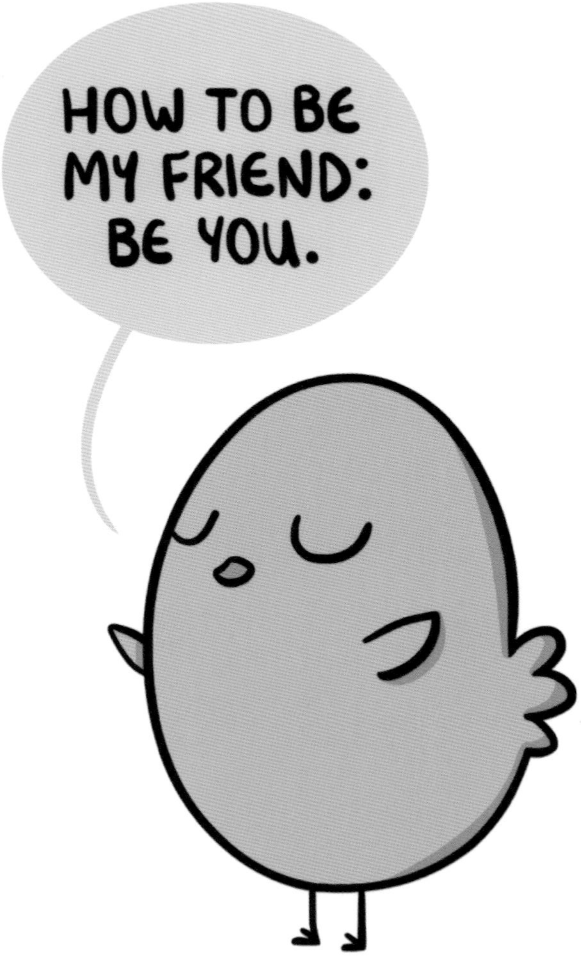
HOW TO BE MY FRIEND: BE YOU.

Positive
Doodles

SORRY IN ADVANCE FOR ALL THE TIME YOU'LL SPEND LISTENING TO ME TALK ABOUT MY NEXT FAVORITE SHOW.

_____

_____

_____

_____

Positive
Doodles

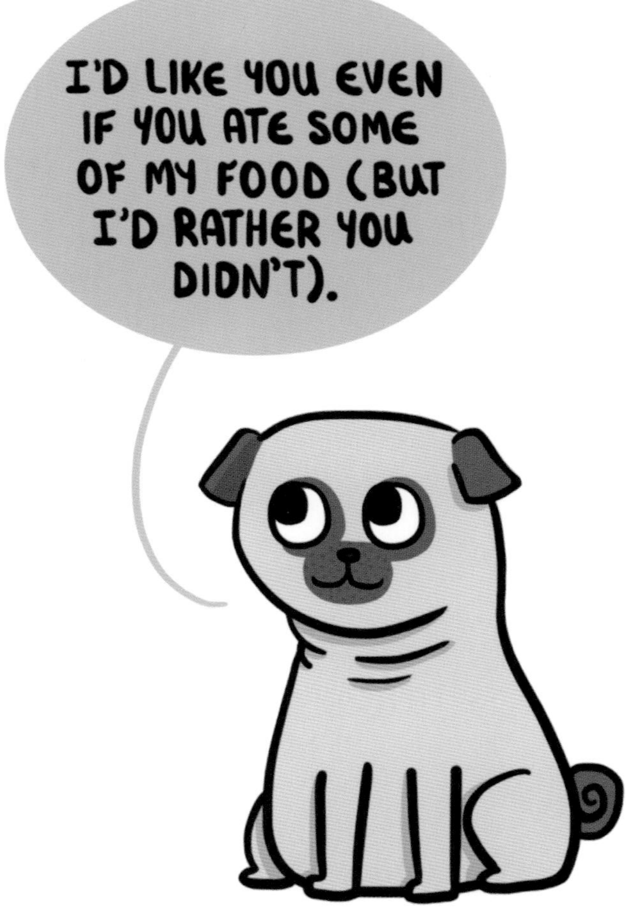
I'D LIKE YOU EVEN IF YOU ATE SOME OF MY FOOD (BUT I'D RATHER YOU DIDN'T).

POSITIVE
DOODLES

NO MATTER HOW
BAD THINGS GET,
BEING AROUND YOU
ALWAYS MAKES ME
FEEL LESS CRABBY.

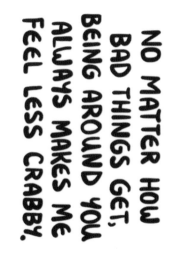

Positive
Doodles

ALL I WANT IS YOUR HAPPINESS... AND TEN MILLION DOLLARS, BUT MOSTLY YOUR HAPPINESS.

POSITIVE
DOODLES

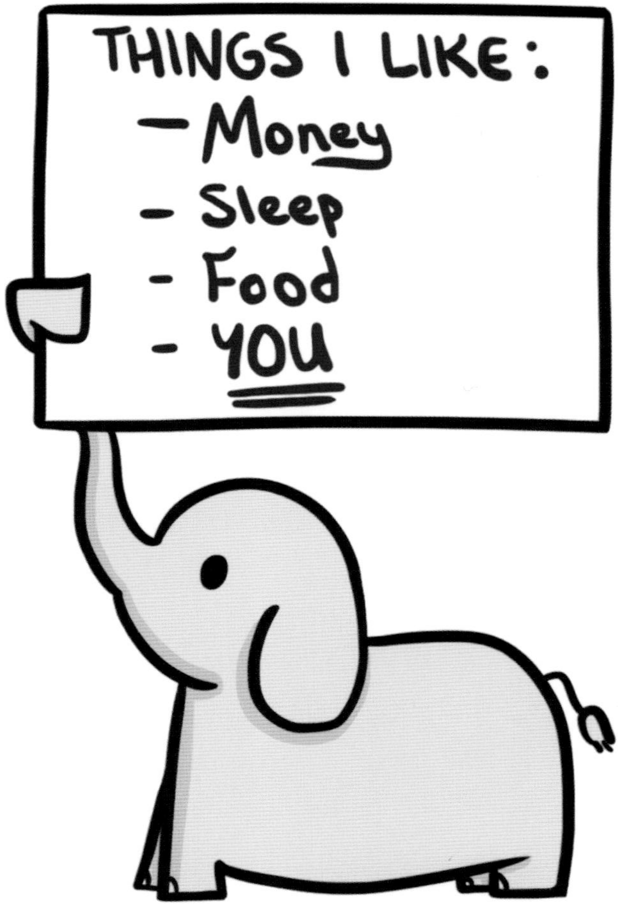
THINGS I LIKE:
– Money
– Sleep
– Food
– YOU

_____

_____

_____

_____

POSITIVE
DOODLES

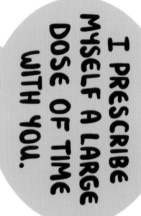

I PRESCRIBE MYSELF A LARGE DOSE OF TIME WITH YOU.

_____

_____

_____

_____

POSITIVE
DOODLES

YOU'RE SO GREAT
I SUSPECT YOU'RE
SECRETLY A ROBOT
PROGRAMMED TO
BE AWESOME.

_____

_____

_____

_____

POSITIVE
DOODLES

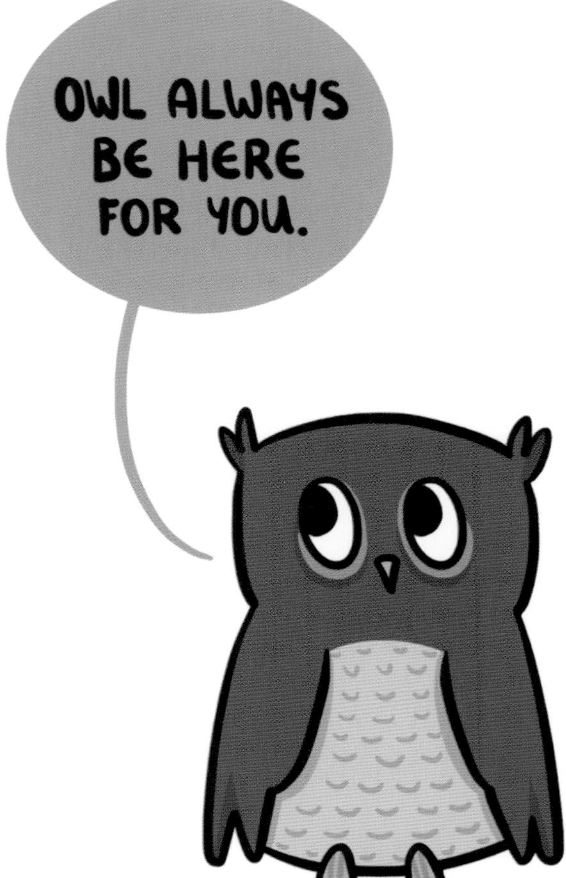
OWL ALWAYS
BE HERE
FOR YOU.

Positive
Doodles

I LOVE THAT I DON'T HAVE TO PRETEND TO BE NORMAL AROUND YOU!

_____

_____

_____

_____

POSITIVE
DOODLES

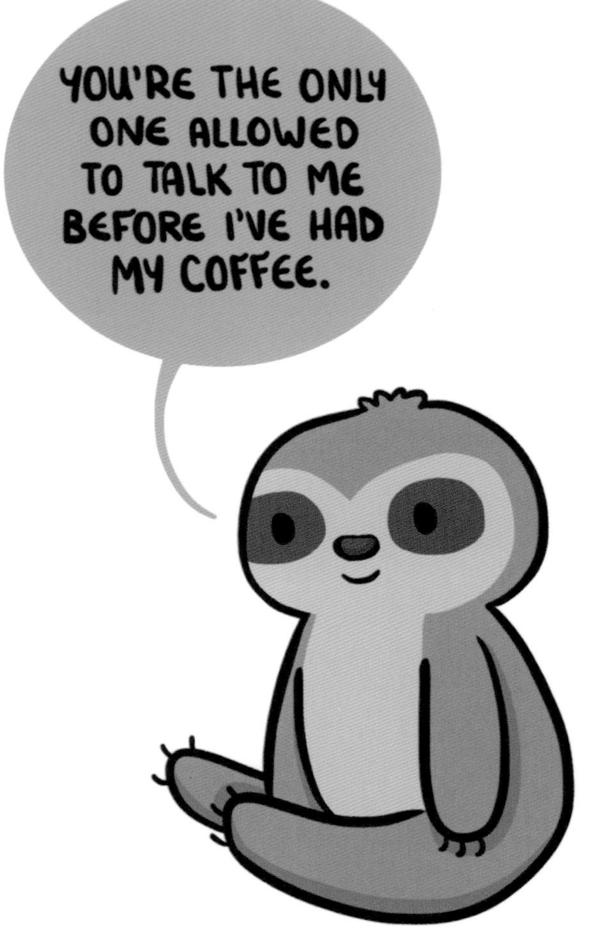
YOU'RE THE ONLY ONE ALLOWED TO TALK TO ME BEFORE I'VE HAD MY COFFEE.

_____

_____

_____

_____

POSITIVE
DOODLES

WE'RE NOT STRANGE, WE'RE JUST... OKAY, WE'RE PRETTY STRANGE, BUT THAT'S WHAT MAKES US INTERESTING.

_____

_____

_____

_____

POSITIVE
DOODLES

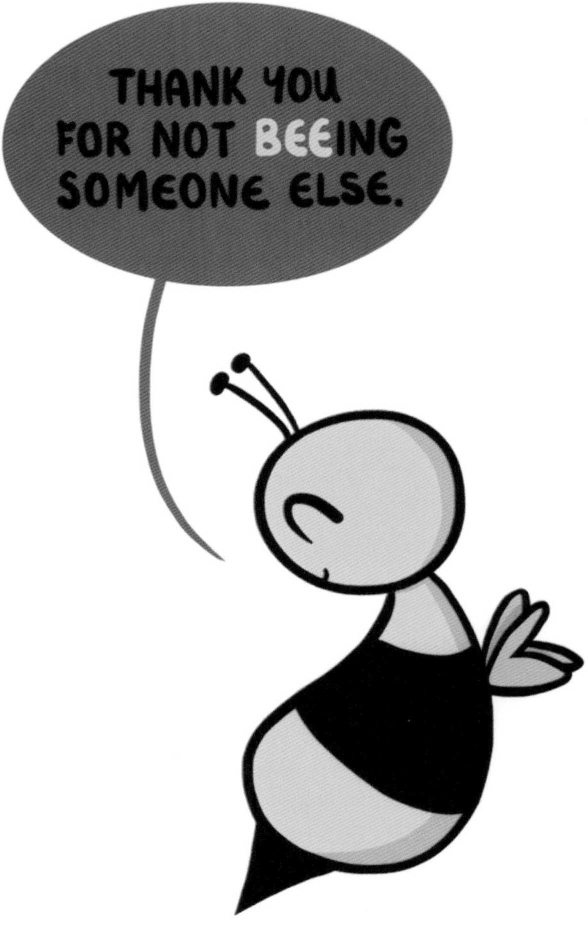
THANK YOU FOR NOT BEEING SOMEONE ELSE.

Positive
Doodles

EVEN WHEN I'M TIRED AND GRUMPY, I'M ALWAYS HAPPY TO SEE YOU.

PositivE
DoodLes

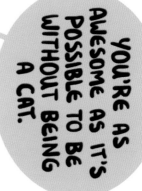

YOU'RE AS AWESOME AS IT'S POSSIBLE TO BE WITHOUT BEING A CAT.

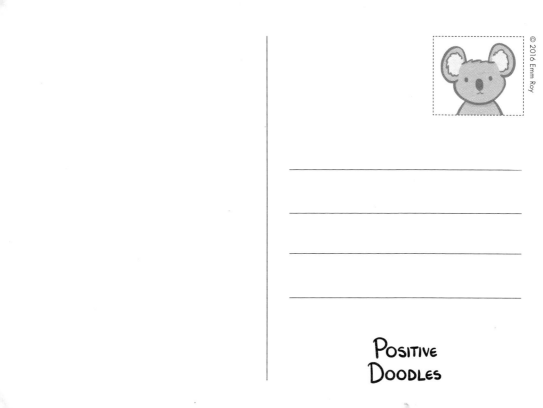

POSITIVE
DOODLES